D0579814

LET'S EXPLORE SCIENCE

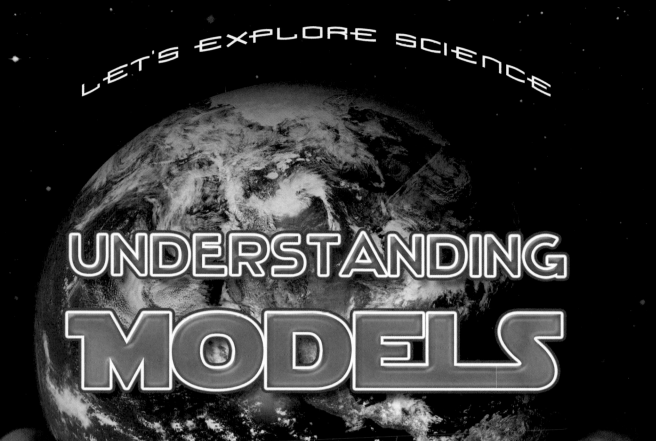

UNDERSTANDING MODELS

AUTHOR
JEANNE STURM

ROURKE PUBLISHING
Vero Beach, Florida 32964

www.rourkepublishing.com

PHOTO CREDITS: © Oleg Prikhodko: Title Page; © Dmitry Mordvintsev: 5; © natsmith1: 6; © NASA: 7; © Knape: 9; © iLexx: 10; © Lockie Currie: 10, 14; © Marcus Clackson: 11; © Klaus Nilkens: 13; © Ahmad Hamoudah: 16; © jan kranendonk: 16; © Jules Katano: 19; © exi5: 21; © Eric Isseleé: 23; © Oleg Koslov: 23; © Martin Valigursky: 23; © Valeria Titova: 23; © Dan Thornberg: 23; © Valeriy Evlakhov: 23; © Paul Whillock: 23; © Nancy Nehring: 23; © MAXFX: 23; © emmgunn: 24; © emanuele ferrari: 25; © appleuzr: 25; © Dave Stevens: 25; © Chris Schmidt: 26; © A-Digit: 27; © Wikipedia: 28, 35; © coepics: 28; © ronen: 29; © Stephanie Horrocks: 29; © Arthur Kwiatkowski: 31; © Alexey Dudoladov: 32; © jacus: 33; © cyrop: 33; © morgan1: 34; © absolut_100: 34; © Jane Norton: 37; © Monique Rodriguez: 40, 41; © Don Nichols: 40; © Serghei Starus: 43; © Dor Jordan: 44; © Rich Legg: 45

Edited by Kelli L. Hicks

Cover and Interior design by Teri Intzegian

Library of Congress Cataloging-in-Publication Data

Sturm, Jeanne.
  Understanding models / Jeanne Sturm.
    p. cm. -- (Let's explore science)
  ISBN 978-1-60694-410-3 (hard cover)
  ISBN 978-1-60694-528-5 (soft cover)
  1. Science--Experiments--Juvenile literature. 2. Models and model making--Juvenile literature. 3. Models (Patterns)--Juvenile literature. I. Title.
  Q182.3.S78 2010
  507.2--dc22

                    2009006084

Printed in the USA

CG/CG

ROURKE PUBLISHING

www.rourkepublishing.com - rourke@rourkepublishing.com
Post Office Box 643328 Vero Beach, Florida 32964

Table of Contents

CHAPTER ONE

Models Help Us Test New Designs

Imagine spending years building a skyscraper, forty floors high. Finally, the last window is set into place and the final piece of tile installed. You plan a grand opening ceremony to unveil your creation to the eager public, but before the big day arrives, a storm blows in. High winds course through the city, and your skyscraper begins to sway in the ever-stronger winds. Finally, incredibly, it comes crashing to the ground.

In Moscow, Russia, old factories were torn down to make room for the Moscow International Business Center. The towers under construction will be 62 and 73 stories when completed.

Your fictional skyscraper was unable to withstand the effects of high wind, but real skyscrapers can. Long before building begins, engineers test their designs in wind tunnels. Airflow in and around the building is studied and analyzed for stability.

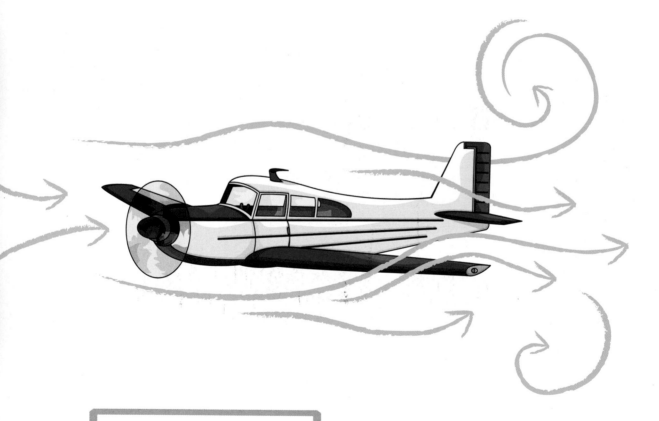

Engineers use a technique called Schlieren photography to study supersonic airflow around aircraft in wind tunnels.

DID YOU KNOW?

NASA uses wind tunnels and water tunnels to test the aerodynamics of vehicles in flight. In water tunnels, blue, red, and green dyes in the water help scientists **predict** how air would flow over an aircraft.

In 1920, the first wind tunnel was built at Langley Research Center. A screened air intake assured a steady flow of air.

The Turning Torso Residential Tower in Malmö, Sweden, is a 54-story skyscraper with a shape distinctly its own. Inspired by the backbone of the human body, the tower twists to mimic the spine of a person twisting his body.

Malmö, Sweden, is an extremely windy place, and the creative design of the tower does not follow the usual time-tested shape for tall buildings, so high winds could have been cause for concern. But residents of the tower have no reason to worry. The building's designers tested a **scale model** of it in a wind tunnel at the University of Western Ontario. Based on these tests, designers predict that even in a storm with a wind force of 98 mph (44 mps), the building would move only 1 foot (30 cm), slowly, at its summit.

The Turning Torso Residential Tower is constructed of nine pentagons stacked on top of each other. From bottom to top, the tower twists 90 degrees.

It was possible to test the strength of the skyscraper using a model in a wind tunnel, allowing the architects of the tower to begin building with confidence. Models help us understand how things work. They help us predict what might happen and plan for the future.

Scale models give planners an idea of how things will fit together.

Designing a building involves preplanning and troubleshooting.

When you think of models, the first thing that comes to mind might be the scale models of cars and airplanes that come in kits. But **scientific models** come in many forms, each useful in a different way. A scientific model is a **representation** of an object or event that we can use to understand the real object or event. We use models when we want to understand something that is too big, too small, or too complex to study.

CHAPTER TWO

Scale Models

Scale models are physical models of an object or system. We usually build them to represent something that is much larger or much smaller than they are. Scale models are **proportional** to the original object. When scaling an object to a smaller size, we scale every part of the object by the same **ratio**. If a dinosaur is being reduced to 1/8 its original size for a museum display, his head, his feet, and his body will all be reduced to 1/8 their original size.

Sometimes it's possible to build a full-scale model. Allosaurs roamed North America 150 million years ago. Though they averaged 30 feet (8.5 meters) in length, scientists believe some were as large as this 39-foot (12-meter) model.

To make a scale model of a large building, you would need to know the **dimensions** of the building—its height, and the length and width of its base. If you wanted to make a scale model of a building that is 800 feet high, with a base 100 feet long and 200 feet wide, you would divide all three dimensions by the same number.

Say you divide all three dimensions by 100. Your scale model would be 8 feet high, 1 foot long, and 2 feet wide. That's a pretty big model. It might be useful for a prop in a play, but you might have wanted something smaller that you could place on a desk or in a shoebox diorama.

Actual Size
800 feet

Scale Model
100 feet = 1 foot

Scale Model
100 feet = 1 inch

You might decide on a scale where 100 feet = 1 inch. To make a scale model of the original building, you would divide all measurements by 100 and change feet to inches.

The original height was 800 feet.

$$\frac{800}{100} = 8$$ The model's height will be 8 inches.

The original length was 100 feet.

$$\frac{100}{100} = 1$$ The model's length will be 1 inch.

The original width was 200 feet.

$$\frac{200}{100} = 2$$ The model's width will be 2 inches.

Your final model is still scaled to the original building, but it is now small enough to use in a diorama.
Note: If you are using metric measurements you are using the same formula.

CHAPTER THREE

Graphical Models

Some models, such as maps and charts, are two-dimensional representations of something. We call these **graphical models**.

Maps are especially helpful when traveling in an unfamiliar city.

Arctic Ocean

Greenland

Greenland Sea
Svalbard
Franz Josef Land
Sevalnaya Zemlya
Kara Sea
Laptev Sea
New Siberian Islands

Baffin Bay

Arctic Circle

Barents Sea
Novaya Zemlya

Iceland
Norwegian Sea
Faroe Islands

Labrador Sea

North Sea

Ural Mountains

Ob

Lake Baikal

Amur

Alps

EUROPE

Volga

Ural

Altay Mountains

Gobi

Land of Newfoundland

Bay of Biscay

Black Sea

Volga

Aral Sea
North Aral Sea

ASIA

Yellow

North Atlantic Ocean

Strait of Gibraltar

Mediterranean Sea

Caspian Sea

Tian

Himalayas

Yangtze

Atlas Mountains

Euphrates

Thar Desert

S a h a r a
D e s e r t

Lake Nasser

Arabian
Peninsula

Arabian Sea

Bay of
Bengal

Ganges

Mekong

Niger

Red Sea

Nile

AFRICA

South
China

Gulf of
Guinea

Congo

Malay
Peninsula

Lake Victoria

Sumatra

Indian Ocean

Java

Madagascar

Mozambique Channel

Kalahari
Desert

South
Atlantic
Ocean

Cape of
Good Hope

? Graphical models like this
map are often used in
schools to help students
learn about the world.

Southern Ocean

Antarctic Circle

Many maps include symbols that represent different things, such as roads, bridges, streams, and campgrounds. A **key** explains the meaning of each symbol that appears on the map.

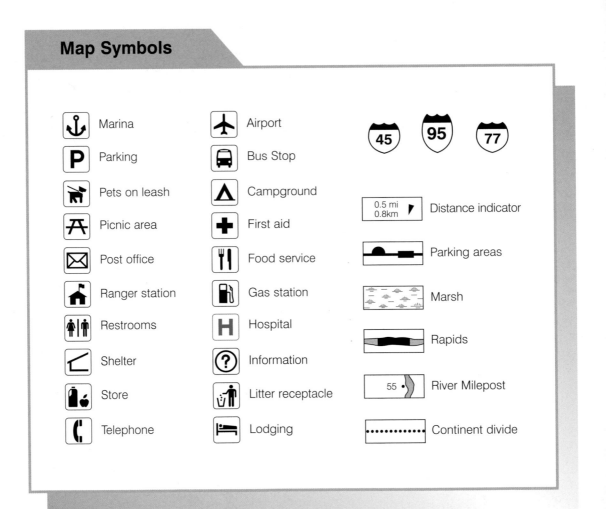

Map Symbols

⚓	Marina	✈	Airport
🅿	Parking	🚌	Bus Stop
	Pets on leash	▲	Campground
	Picnic area	✚	First aid
✉	Post office	🍴	Food service
	Ranger station		Gas station
	Restrooms	H	Hospital
	Shelter	?	Information
	Store		Litter receptacle
	Telephone		Lodging

45 95 77

0.5 mi
0.8km ▶ Distance indicator

Parking areas

Marsh

Rapids

55 ● River Milepost

Continent divide

If you are traveling in the car and looking for a rest area along the highway, you would look for a specific symbol that represents a rest area on your map.

An airplane symbol helps travelers locate the closest airport.

You might want to know how far it is from your home to the library. On your map, it looks like it is just a few centimeters from one to the other. But what does this mean? You need to find the scale of your map.

Somewhere, off to the side, you will see a line that looks like a ruler. It will be in either customary or metric units. Using the scale on the map, it might tell you that 2 centimeters equals 1 kilometer. You can use this information to calculate how far it is from one place to another.

$$\frac{\text{Distance on the Map}}{\text{Distance on the Ground}} = \frac{2 \text{ cm}}{1 \text{ km}} = \frac{2 \text{ cm}}{100,000 \text{ cm}} = \frac{1 \text{ cm}}{50,000 \text{ cm}}$$

On a particular map, 2 centimeters on the map represent 1 actual kilometer. Since 1 kilometer equals 100,000 centimeters, we can go on to say that the 2 centimenters on the map represent 100,000 actual centimeters. If we divide both numberes by 2, we find that the map is drawn to a scale of 1 to 50,000 (1:50,000).

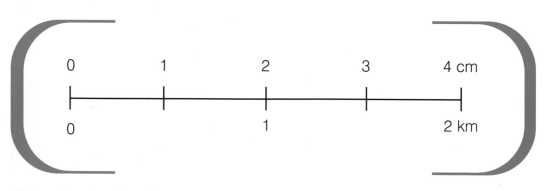

This scale, taken from the map on page 21, converts centimeters to kilometers.

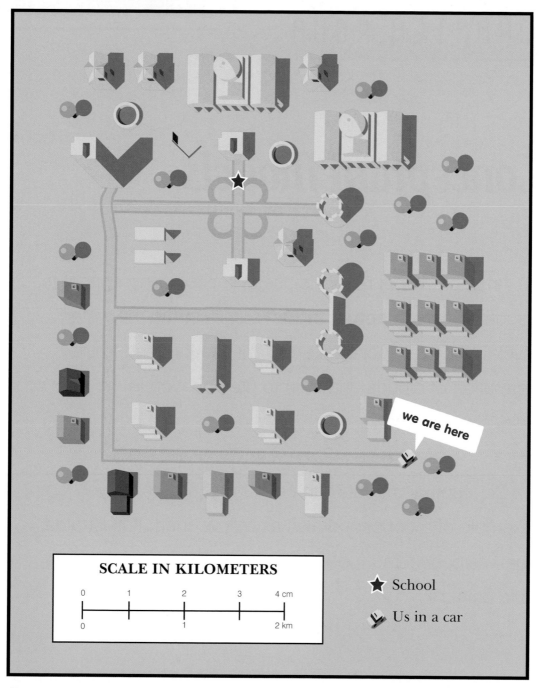

SCALE IN KILOMETERS

0   1   2   3   4 cm

0   1   2 km

★ School

Us in a car

You can use a ruler, a piece of paper, or even the length of your finger to find out how far it is from place to place on this map. How many kilometers would you drive to get to school?

CHAPTER FOUR

Conceptual Models

Another kind of model is useful in explaining concepts, or ideas. A **conceptual model** can illustrate the water cycle, where evaporation and transpiration lead to the formation of clouds and then to precipitation in the form of rain, sleet, or snow.

Conceptual models can be diagrams. A food web is an example of a concept drawn as a flow chart. It illustrates the interconnected food chains in a community of plants and animals.

Each link in the food chain depends on another plant or animal for the survival of its species.

A Terrestrial Food Chain

Hawk

Snake

Rat

Grasshopper

Plant

A Marine Food Chain

Bear

Salmon

Perch

Zooplankton

Phytoplankton

Conceptual models can even be verbal descriptions or drawings of how something works. It's easier to explain why we have different seasons when we can see how the tilt of the Earth changes over the course of a year. In June, July, and August, when the Northern Hemisphere tilts toward the Sun, it experiences summer as it receives direct rays that bring more warmth. At the same time, the Southern Hemisphere, tilted away from the Sun and receiving indirect rays, is experiencing winter.

THE SEASONS ON EARTH

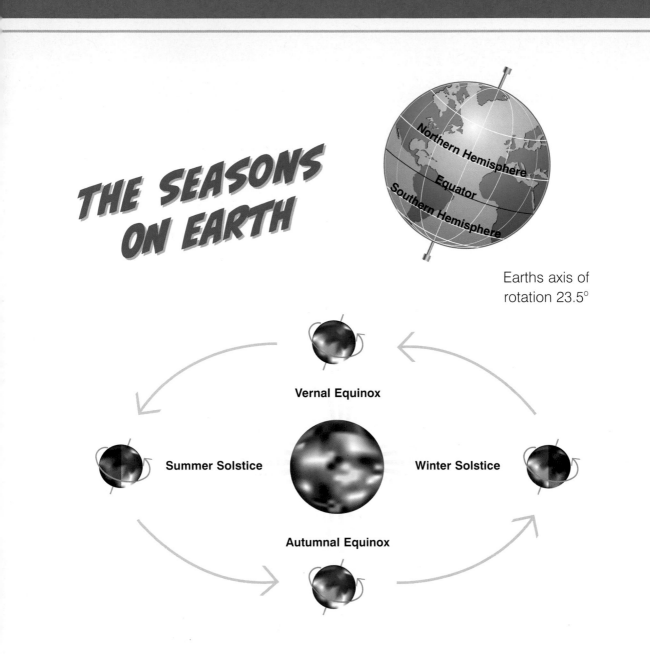

Northern Hemisphere
Equator
Southern Hemisphere

Earths axis of rotation 23.5°

Vernal Equinox

Summer Solstice

Winter Solstice

Autumnal Equinox

Vernal Equinox:
The vernal equinox is the first day of spring in the Northern Hemisphere.

Autumnal Equinox:
The autumnal equinox is the first day of autumn in the Northern Hemisphere.

Summer Solstice:
The summer solstice is the first day of summer in the Northern Hemisphere.

Winter Solstice:
The winter solstice is the first day of winter in the Northern Hemisphere.

CHAPTER FIVE

Mathematical Models

A **mathematical model** is an equation that illustrates the way a process works. We can use a mathematical model to calculate how a country's population will grow over time. Engineering, statistics, and computer science are among the many fields that employ mathematical models in their work.

Engineering students put their ideas into practice.

The study of physics relies on mathematical models. Newton's 2nd Law of Motion can be expressed mathematically as F=ma (Force = mass x acceleration). You might experiment with this law by comparing the force needed to push an empty shopping cart compared to one that is full of groceries. The mass of the cart increases as you add more food. The amount of force necessary to move an empty shopping cart is much smaller than that needed to move a full one, and even more force is necessary to move a full cart quickly out of the way of an absentminded shopper coming your way!

2nd Law of Motion
F=ma

Acceleration is quick with a light load. Less force is needed.

A large load makes for slower acceleration. Bringing the cart to a stop will be more difficult, too.

In most fields of study, different types of models are used to fill different needs. Weather models, for example, can be graphical, mathematical, or conceptual. A mathematical model can tell you what chance there is of rain on a given day. A graphical model can show approaching cold or warm fronts on a map and warn of dangerous storms on the way. A conceptual model can explain long-term weather trends, showing how current conditions might be drier or cooler than the average for an area.

A dual monitor work station allows a meteorologist to take information from both graphical and conceptual weather models.

Local forecasters give us an idea of how approaching weather fronts will affect our plans.

CHAPTER SIX

Computer Models

A **computer model**, or **simulation**, is one type of mathematical model. Computer simulations are used in many fields of science, including physics, chemistry, biology, and economics, as well as in technology, entertainment, and business.

We use computer models to predict where air pollutants in the atmosphere will go. In the event of a chlorine spill, for example, computer models can tell emergency personnel where chlorine gas fumes will be carried by the wind. Then, people can evacuate the area until the air clears.

Computer simulation is used in flight simulators to train pilots, in traffic engineering to plan or redesign traffic flow, and in modeling car crashes to test safety mechanisms in new vehicle models.

DID YOU KNOW?

Pilots train on flight simulators programmed to mimic real-life experiences. They can learn to handle different types of aircraft and practice their responses to emergency situations that might crop up during an actual flight.

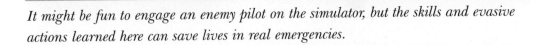

It might be fun to engage an enemy pilot on the simulator, but the skills and evasive actions learned here can save lives in real emergencies.

In simulated car crashes, computer models study the effects of force and motion on the car and on the passengers inside. Long before automakers build the final prototype of a new car, computer simulations have allowed them to precisely test the effects of a crash and make changes based on their results. Lifesaving devices have been built into cars because of the knowledge engineers have gained through studying the effects of car crashes.

Crash tests give us an idea of how well a vehicle will protect its occupants in an accident.

DID YOU KNOW?

When they were first developed, crash test dummies were all the same size, weight, and shape. Now, they come in all shapes and sizes, and include pregnant women, small children, and infants. In a crash that takes place in less than a second, engineers can gather information from points throughout the model's body, then download it to a computer where it will be analyzed and used to develop safer cars.

Even with the benefits of computer modeling, automakers haven't stopped subjecting actual cars to crash tests, in part because they value the wealth of information they get from crash test dummies. Crash test dummies have been in use for decades, supplying engineers with detailed information about the effects of sudden impact on the human body.

CHAPTER SEVEN

Models in Astronomy

Models of the solar system show the positions of the planets and their moons as they orbit the Sun. While these models are useful in comparing the sizes of the planets and moons, it is difficult to build them to scale. Distances between planets are huge compared to the size of the planets.

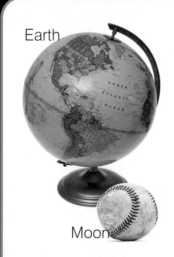

Earth

Moon

If you stood by Epcot's geosphere holding a baseball in one hand and a globe in the other, you would see a scale model of the differences in the sizes of the real objects. However, it wouldn't be a scale model for the distances between the objects. To make a scale model for both the sizes and the distances, you would need to stand 3 miles (4.8 kilometers) away from the geosphere, holding the globe, and then you would need a friend to stand 40 feet (12 meters) from you, holding a baseball.

Think of the globe in your classroom. Most classroom globes are 16 inches (41 centimeters) in **diameter**. If you made a model of the solar system and used the classroom globe as your Earth, our Moon would be about the size of a baseball, with a diameter of 4 inches (10 centimeters).

Remaining consistent in your scale, the Sun would have to be 146 feet (44.6 meters) in diameter, a little smaller than the diameter of the geosphere at Epcot Center in Florida.

Sun

Another model, using a different scale, would make it easier to view the distance from the Sun to Pluto all at once. If you placed the Sun on one goal line of a football field, Pluto's position would be on the opposite goal line, 100 yards (91.4 meters) away. Earth would sit 2.5 yards (2.3 meters) away from the Sun. This model gives a better understanding of the relative distance from the Sun to each planet, ending at Pluto. But the reduced scale of this model makes it necessary to reduce the size of the Sun and planets as well. No longer the size of a classroom globe, in this scale the Earth would have a diameter of 0.008 inch (0.2 millimeters). Even the Sun would be smaller than one inch wide. Its diameter would measure 0.85 inches (21.5 millimeters).

Sitting in the stands of the football stadium, we wouldn't even be able to see the Sun and the tiny planets. But if we placed a stake in the ground at each planet's position, we could at least get an idea of where they would be, and we would have a better understanding of the immensity of our solar system.

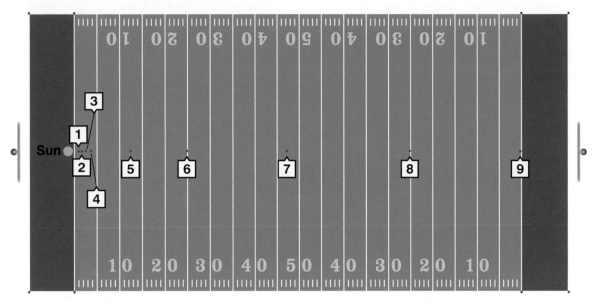

AU stands for astronomical unit. It is the distance from the center of the Earth to the center of the Sun. In this scale model, it is 2.5 yards (2.3 meters), but a true AU is 93 million miles (149.6 million kilomters).

Planets Distance from the Sun

		AU	Yards	Meters
1	Mercury	.40	1.0	.91
2	Venus	.70	1.75	1.6
3	Earth	1	2.5	2.3
4	Mars	1.5	3.75	3.4
5	Jupiter	5	12.5	11.4
6	Saturn	10	25	22.9
7	Uranus	19	47.50	43.
8	Neptune	30	75	68.6
9	Pluto	40	100	91.4

CHAPTER EIGHT

Models Help Us Understand Living Things

A stalk of celery can model the process of capillary action, by which plants conduct water from their roots to their leaves. Place a freshly cut stalk of celery in a glass of water that has been tinted with red food coloring. After a few hours, you will be able to see the red liquid in the veins of the plant. You can trace the path of the water as it makes its way from the stem to the leaves of the celery stalk.

RED CELERY EXPERIMENT

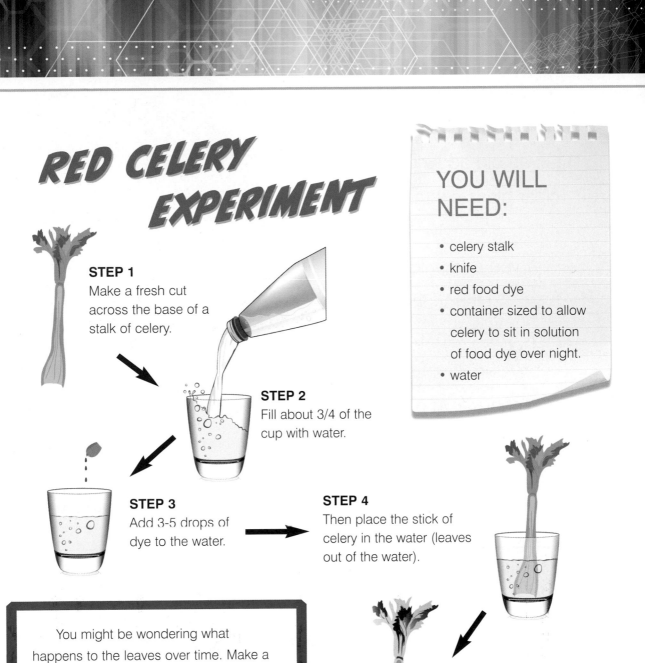

STEP 1
Make a fresh cut across the base of a stalk of celery.

STEP 2
Fill about 3/4 of the cup with water.

STEP 3
Add 3-5 drops of dye to the water.

STEP 4
Then place the stick of celery in the water (leaves out of the water).

STEP 5
After a few days the celery will change colors!

YOU WILL NEED:

- celery stalk
- knife
- red food dye
- container sized to allow celery to sit in solution of food dye over night.
- water

You might be wondering what happens to the leaves over time. Make a cut across the celery stem and use a hand lens to observe. If you look carefully, you will see tiny red vessels that carried the food coloring to the top of the stalk.

A terrarium is a great way to model an ecosystem. You can build a terrarium in a gallon jar, an old aquarium, or any clear glass container.

If you add a lid to make a closed terrarium you'll have your own miniature ecosystem in a self-sustaining greenhouse. At night, plants use oxygen and release carbon dioxide. In the daytime, during photosynthesis, plants use the carbon dioxide and release oxygen and water vapor. The water vapor stays trapped within the system, creating moisture for the plants.

Small gravel and moss placed on top of the soil helps retain moisture.

CHAPTER NINE

Models Help Us Understand Things Too Small to See

Plant and animal cells are too small to see without a microscope, but we can make a model of a cell. One fun idea is to use different foods for the different structures of the cell. Gelatin can act as the cytoplasm. If you pour gelatin into a container and refrigerate it until it is almost set (about an hour), it will be the perfect medium to hold all the cell components in place.

You can use different candies and fruits to represent all the different parts of the cell. Be sure to make a list of what each food item represents. After you show your creation to someone, it might make a yummy treat.

If this were a cell, the yellow gelatin is acting like the cytoplasm of a cell and the items within are the parts of the cell.

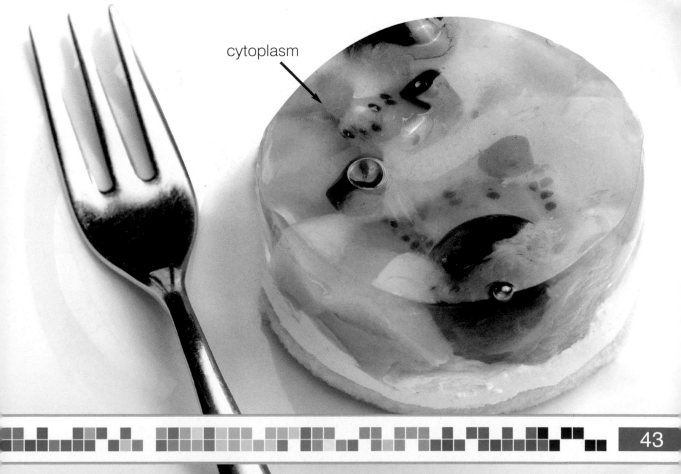

cytoplasm

Models represent objects or systems in ways that make it easier for us to comprehend them.

We might use physical models to understand microscopic cells, conceptual models to understand our place in a food web, or mathematical models to predict the global population in 20 years. Whichever type we choose, models help us understand and explain our complex world.

Radio-controlled aircraft are not only popular with hobbyists and scientists, but effective models for understanding flight.

GLOSSARY

computer model (kuhm-PYOO-tur MOD-uhl): a computer program that is used to model something

conceptual model (kuhn-SEP-shu-uhl MOD-uhl): a written or illustrated explanation of how something works

diameter (dye-AM-uh-tur): a line segment that passes through the center of a circle and has endpoints on the circle

dimensions (duh-MEN-shuhnz): the length, width, and height of an object

graphical models (GRAF-ik-uhl MOD-uhls): two-dimensional representations of something

key (KEE): a chart that explains the symbols on a map

mathematical model (math-uh-MAT-ik-uhl MOD-uhl): an equation or equations that shows how a system or process works

predict (pri-DIKT): to say what you think will happen

proportional (pruh-POR-shuhn-uhl): having the same ratio

ratio (RAY-shee-oh): a comparison of two amounts using division

representation (rep-ri-zen-TA-shuhn): pictures or models that stand for something else

scale model (SKALE MOD-uhl): proportional models of an object

scientific models (SYE-uhn-TIF-ik MOD-uhlz): representations of an object or event that help us understand the real object or event

simulation (sim-yuh-LAY-shuhn): a model of an experiment

Index

Websites to Visit

www.exploratorium.edu/ronh/solar_system

www.sciencephoto.com/html_tech_archive/schlie.html

starchild.gsfc.nasa.gov/docs/StarChild/StarChild.html

About the Author

Jeanne Sturm grew up exploring the woods, waterfalls, and riverbanks around her home in Chagrin Falls, Ohio. She earned her education degree at Bowling Green State University and moved to Tampa, Florida, to teach. She began windsurfing, where she met her future husband. Now married, Jeanne, her husband, and their three children live in Land O' Lakes, Florida, with their dog, Astro.